Comments from Readers of Jack's April Fool's and Other Humour Columns

I haven't had such a good laugh in a long time.

Growing up for you was just never an option! Keep having fun.

I had a good laugh at this one - still wiping away the tears!

I like your sense of humour!

Jack, you got me again. I can't believe I voted for you!

That was great. I laughed all the way through.

My wife just paid you one of the highest compliments an Aussie can make to anyone: She said, "Jack Popjes is a nut!"

Keep us thinking, Jack, and laughing!!

A Tickle in the Funny Bone

Cheers! Jack

" a merry heart doeth good, like a medicine " should

Prov. 17:22

Jack Popjes

TheWordMan Ministries

The WordMan

A Tickle in the Funny Bone

Cover Design by Randy Hayashi
Formatting by Wild Seas Formatting
(http://www.WildSeasFormatting.com)

ISBN-13: 978-1543116823

ISBN-10: 1543116825

The WordMan

Author's Preface

There are two occasions when we refer to our funny bone. One, when we knock the ulnar nerve in our elbow against some hard object and, as we experience a sharp, tingling sensation, we grimace and exclaim, "Ai! I just hit my funny bone!"

The other is when something strikes us as comical and we say, "That tickles my funny bone."

I don't know why the ulnar nerve is called the funny bone since striking it against something hard is not a funny experience, except possibly to observers of the inevitable grimaces that follows.

The thirteen columns in this book have tickled the funny bones of many of those who read them in my blogs. And, yes, some of the April Fool's tricks no doubt resulted in grimaces of chagrin when they realized I had tricked them once again.

The title of this book, *A Tickle in the Funny Bone,* is designed to counterbalance the previously published three books of story-based articles with physically abusive titles, *A Poke in the Ribs*, *A Kick in the Pants*, and *A Bonk on the Head*.

History of April Fool's Tricks

Fooling friends and relatives on the first of April is a long-standing tradition in the Netherlands where I was born. I have a vivid memory of walking 20 minutes to school when I was probably in grade one or two, and panicking when I found the schoolyard empty.

I was late! Oh no! I ran to the school door. It was locked! I rang the bell and when the janitor opened it, I tried to worm my way in saying,

"Ik ben laat!" (I'm late!) but he replied,

"Nee, je bent te vroeg." (No, you're too early.) He pulled his watch from his vest pocket and showed me. Sure enough, I was an hour early.

I trudged back home, and my Mom was startled to see me appear and asked if I was sick. I told her I was an hour early. "That can't be, look at the clock. It's past school time."

That's when my Dad walked in grinning from ear to ear saying, "April Fool," as he turned the clock back one hour. While waiting for the real time to go to school he told me the history behind the custom of tricking people on April 1.

During the 80-year's war between the Protestant Netherlands and Roman Catholic Spain, the Dutch prince William of Orange, a national hero, led the long revolt against Spanish occupation under the cruel yoke of the duke of Alva. Under Alva's reign of terror countless Protestant Christians were persecuted and martyred.

William could not fight on land since he was totally outnumbered by the Spanish troops, but on the sea the hundreds of small fishing vessels he led fought bravely against the massive Spanish galleons, sinking some of them. The Spanish occupiers contemptuously called them Sea Beggars.

The turning point finally came on April 1, 1572, when several hundred hungry Dutch fighters in small ships sailed up the river to the city of Den Brielle to look for food. When the ferryman, who was secretly in sympathy with the freedom fighters, reported the approaching flotilla to the Spanish authorities in the city, they asked, "How many Sea Beggars are there?"

"Oh, probably about 5,000," he replied.

Such a large number frightened the authorities who, with all the occupying Spanish soldiers, fled the city. That day the Dutch freedom fighters took the city of Den Brielle without a fight. The following week the city of Vlissingen was also liberated by the troops of William of Orange. That was the beginning of the end of Spain's domination of the Netherlands.

The city name Brielle or Brille, sounds like the word *bril*, meaning glasses. As a child I learned the rhyme, *Op één april verloor Alva zijn bril!* "On the first of April, Alva lost his glasses."

The ferryman's lie told on April 1, tricking the Spanish oppressors 450 years ago, is commemorated even today, not only in the Netherlands, but in many other countries and cultures all over the world.

Being loyal to my Dutch heritage I, therefore, committed myself to trick as many people as I could on April 1. What better way than through my weekly emailed blog postings to Wycliffe members and my friends and supporters.

Many readers who subscribed in later years have lamented that they missed earlier April Fool's columns. To make up for this grievous disappointment, here are seven years' worth of April Fool's tricks, each one followed by the oft times hilarious comments and responses of the readers.

Have fun.

April 1,

A Dusty Audio Tape Leads to a Startling Discovery

I admit it. I am a packrat. I keep stuff for years and eventually have to do a cleanup and toss out most of it. But last week was a notable exception. Most notable!

While rummaging through some old Canela language papers, I found a small dusty box of old audio cassettes — recordings of legends I had taped back in the late 1960's at the start of our education and Bible translation ministry among the Canela people of Brazil. We had used some of the stories to analyse the Canela language, while we turned others into easy reading booklets.

Just for old times' sake, I inserted a cassette into my player. As I listened to the now long-dead Canela village elder tell one of the myths about origins of Canela customs, I realized I had never heard this story before. I listened fascinated as he told of the reason for the unique circular layout of Canela villages. From the air, they look like gigantic wagon wheels. The central plaza is the wheel hub, the houses stand around the rim road facing inward, and paths radiate out from the plaza to each house, just like spokes in a wheel.

People who see an aerial photo of Canela villages always ask, "Why do they design their villages like this?" Well, here, at last, is the official answer:

"Many generations ago," the old narrator began, "our forefathers lived very differently. They didn't know how to make fire so they ate their food raw. They didn't know how to prepare manioc root or build houses. They hunted with clubs only since they didn't know how to make bows and arrows. They lived in small family groups here and there in temporary shelters under the trees.

"One day they heard a great booming, roaring noise, like a prolonged thunder. Then total silence. Stealthily the bravest men from each family group sneaked towards the place where the noise had come from. There, in an open area, they saw it—a huge gourd, or cucumber but shiny and white, standing straight on end. They watched from their hiding places, as six people climbed out of a hole in the side of the gourd, carrying bags. They took things out of those bags and left them lying on the ground on the edge of the open area. Then they climbed back into the great white gourd and closed the opening.

"Our ancestors waited until dark, then quickly slipped out of their hiding places and grabbed the things the gourd visitors had left there. They had never seen things like these before—baskets, bows and arrows, stones with very sharp edges and all kinds of things that smelled, and tasted, good.

"Every day, the visitors came out and, giving more gifts, made friends with our ancestors. They stayed for many moons, learning our language and teaching our ancestors how to weave baskets from palm leaves, how to make fire, and roast meat and roots. Yes, that is how our forefathers learned how to build houses, and make bows and arrows and hunt with them. Until then they didn't even know how to make stone axes.

"Our ancestors loved the gourd people and were very sad when they had to leave. The gourd people told them they should stand far away because of the fire. All the visitors climbed back into their shiny white gourd and closed the hole in the side. Then a great fire spurted out from the bottom of the gourd and with a great roar the gourd rose into the sky and disappeared. It never came back.

"Our ancestors ran to where it had been standing, and saw a great open circle all burned off. In many places the fire had reached beyond the circle and burned paths radiating outwards. They decided to build their houses around the great circle, and walk on the paths towards the centre each day to meet and talk about what they had learned from their visitors.

"And that is why," concluded the old narrator, "we Canela people shape our villages the way we do, and meet in the central plaza to talk and tell stories every day."

*Check out a satellite picture on Google Earth in these coordinates: 6*04'43.39 South, 45*08'48.08 West)

Now before you forward this story to the SETI Institute (Intelligence Search for Extra Terrestrials), please note the date at the top of this column.

***

Responses to A Dusty Audio Tape Leads to a Startling Discovery

Jack, I was really impressed with your latest column. In fact, so much so that I was beginning to wonder *Is this stuff really true?* I should have been more alert to the date and who was writing. However, gullible me had to keep reading to the end until your "heads up" reminded me of the date and its significance. One day I'll be ready, but until then please keep adding the "heads up" statements at the end of these special messages. They may be the only things that keep some of us from jumping to some very big conclusions. P.

P. You wouldn't believe the large number of Wycliffe members, supporters and others who did NOT catch on, even with the heads up on the date at the end. It is scary. Some of these people are translating Bibles! Jack

***

I felt my credulity being stretched but confess that it was

not till I read your reference to the date, that the penny dropped. So what is the real reason for the circular layout? – I know, they have been watching too many 'Wagon Wheel' reruns! RT

***

G'day Jack! My wife just paid you one of the highest compliments an Aussie can make to anyone: She said, "Jack Popjes is a nut!" And I'm more than minutely pleased that I twigged to this being an April Fool's joke at least halfway thro' it! Can't fool this old fool! Cheers, Mate! B

***

Why do I not catch on to your messages on April 1! You got me again. S

***

Tsk, tsk. I wonder if that is how the book *Chariots of the Gods* was written? It caused quite a sensation at the time, was supposed to be scientific. But then, I heard the author interviewed and he admitted it was a form of Germanic fiction writing – not quite fiction, but not quite fact either. Blessings, Jack. Keep us thinking -- and laughing!! SH

***

Awesome story. We could probably use some gourd people visitations here too. I'm sure they could teach us a lot. TS

***

We enjoy your articles, but this one has us buffaloed!! Please explain — what was the date? Obviously, the story sounds like some kind of space machine in an experimental stage. Has it been verified? Just curious. LA

***

Okay, I checked out the date, now what?? I hate to admit it, but I don't get the significance of the date. But, I sure enjoyed the story!! BG

Hi LA & B. Do you not have an April 1, April Fool's tradition in your background? Jack

***

That is hilarious. I looked all over your email for a date of this gourd story but never thought to look at today's date! You are such a kick. SW

***

When you mentioned a great fire spurting out from the bottom of the great gourd I began to think something was a little fishy about this story. At first, I was thinking maybe this was a helicopter but wasn't this supposed to have taken place in more ancient times? Then as I read on I began to wonder about your sanity. Thanks for the laugh. L :)

***

Great story Jack!!! And thanks for the reminder that it is April 1st!! H&D

***

Ha ha ha ha ha! Happy April 1 to you too Jack! L

***

Well.... I was getting *sussy as I read along. You're such

a good story teller and it was a very plausible story - as tribal legends go, I guess. But when I got to the end I had a good laugh and thought "typical!!!" Sister Annie

*Sussy -- Aussie word, for suspicious

Degrees Pay Off in Wycliffe

Every year thousands of people from Western countries, including missionaries of every kind, apply for visas to work in developing countries, and every year many of these applications are denied. Why? Most of these potential workers are not academically qualified. Many developing countries now routinely demand at least a Master's degree in the foreign worker's area of expertise before they will grant a working visa.

Because of the relatively modest educational standards of some mission agencies, they have been effectively shut out of these countries. This is, of course, not as big a problem for Wycliffe, since our thousands of members worldwide probably have more advanced educational degrees per capita than all other mission agencies combined.

This is not surprising. After all, pioneer linguistic research in unwritten languages, and a strong emphasis on training nationals, demands high educational standards. Even so, a few years ago, Wycliffe Bible Translators pioneered an incentive program to encourage its members to upgrade their personal academic degrees. The leadership felt that with the ever-increasing cost of higher education nowadays some form of incentive was needed.

One notable exception to the "high cost problem" is the Canada Institute of Linguistics CanIL) on the campus of Trinity Western University in Langley BC. It is still the best place to get the most "bang for your buck" in linguistic education. CanIL President Dr. Mike Walrod said that the fact that students have come to CanIL from thirty different countries confirms this.

During a recent two-month stay in San Jose, California, I interviewed a Wycliffe colleague, Dr. A. Paul Fuhl, in his home in nearby Palo Florie. He was the architect of the higher education incentive plan and was delighted to explain how it worked and what the results have been.

For the past seventy years, Wycliffe organizations have expected all their member workers to raise their own financial support. All Wycliffe workers have agreed to let Wycliffe assess their income by 10%. This is historic and traditional. The 10% provides administrative services to the workers both at home and on the field. All Wycliffe's financial supporters know this and agree to this system.

What is not as well known, however, is that for the past few years some Wycliffe missionaries are *not* assessed the full 10%. The assessment is reduced according to the following scale of educational achievements:

A Bachelor's degree earns the holder a 1% discount, thus he is assessed, not 10% but 9%. A Master's degree earns a 2% discount. A Doctorate, a 5% discount. Some linguist/translators have multiple degrees, and further discounts are earned by graduating with distinctions such as *magna cum laude*, and *summa cum laude*, etc. One highly educated genius is not only not assessed, she actually receives a 3% bonus.

The biblical basis for this incentive program is provided by wise king Solomon, "A feast is made for laughter, and wine maketh merry: but money answereth all things." Or as *The Message* has it, ". . . but it's money that makes the world go around" (Ecclesiastes 10:19).

Wycliffe's international administration is pleased with the results of this program thus far. Large numbers of Wycliffe workers are upgrading their academic degrees, studying either full time or part time. Relatively soon, lack of academic degrees will not stand in the way of receiving visas to any country in the world.

As far as I know, no other mission agency in the world has an educational incentive program such as Wycliffe's. Once again, Wycliffe proves that its slogan, "We Pioneer" is justified.

Further information on this incentive is available on Wycliffe websites, or by calling the Associated Public Relations Information Line (APRIL) For Outside Operation Listings (FOOL)

***

Responses to Degrees Pay Off in Wycliffe

This one was quite clever -- you had me going till the very last line. I was about to email Wycliffe USA and ask why I was not getting all these discounts!! :-) B

***

I have been reading your weekly e-mail reflections for several years and find them very well-written thought-provoking and worth passing on (hope that's O.K.). I was very interested to hear about the Wycliffe Incentive program. Is that just a program from Wycliffe Canada or is that being used across the board? Or are you pulling our legs again? I've had a Ph.D. since 1981 and have never received a discount on my 10% assessment as far as I know. If this is for real, who should I contact to ask about it? Thanks for your help. HM (PhD)

HM, I think I Gotcha! Jack

***

Ecclesiastes 10:19 (NIV) is my birthday verse! Seemed very appropriate when I was director of development for WBT US. I wondered why it was mailed Friday instead of Saturday. Even in hot northern Thailand we notice the little things.:) FV

***

Nice try, Jack! Even though it was April 2 our time when you sent it, I realised it was something to do with April 1! B

Hi F & B, For date sensitive e-mail messages, such my last Look, you'd think our IT department would figure out some sort of graduated release of messages depending on the international time zone of the recipient. Maybe someday. In the meantime, we muddle along the best we can. Jack

***

Very good Jack. You sucked me in until I got to the last paragraph. BW

***

Great message, Jack. You had me reading eagerly to the very end! DBS (PhD)

***

So Jack, is it any coincidence that it is April 1? I like this idea actually. BM

***

I assume that the incentive program only applies to Americans. I have an MA, but still pay the 10%! Or maybe it is only for the newcomers, not us old timers. HH

HH, You need to do two things, 1) check the date my incentive column was written, and 2) carefully read the last line of the column. Jack

***

I note the date is April 1! I hope others do too or Wycliffe finance offices will be VERY busy answering questions! BM

***

You are a great encourager of creative writing! M

***

We are not all wet behind the ears. Happy April Fool's Day. T&M

***

How much percentage do you get off your 10% assessment! Ha, ha! SC

SC, I am a high school dropout, so I am assessed 11%! Ha, ha! Jack

April 1

A Brilliant Solution

A good board meeting does at least two things for a CEO. First, in the weeks before board meetings, he is focused on producing a good overview of the total organization to present to the board. Then, during the weeks after the board meetings, he is focused on finding creative solutions to the problems that surfaced. Last week's Wycliffe Canada board meetings in our office followed this proven formula.

This past week our leadership team struggled with two familiar problems, how to recruit more people into Bible translation, and how to raise current member financial support. You all know how, after you have focused hard on certain problems and then take time to relax, your brain suddenly and spontaneously brings up solutions to, thus far, insoluble problems. Such was also the case this week. The problems of recruitment and member financial support, it turns out, can actually work together to solve each other.

But first, some background information: Some people are natural recruiters, but they are not many, and even fewer people are natural fund raisers. But, as is often the case, with some outside incentive many of us could do much better in both areas. That is why the solution below is so brilliant. It provides a welcome fiscal incentive to members to recruit, which in turn is paid for by the funds raised by the one who is recruited. Here's how it works:

Let's say a typical financially under-supported missionary, working under this scheme, comes home on furlough and recruits someone into the mission organization, answering his questions, helping him fill in his application papers, and mentoring him through the process. Once the candidate has been accepted into membership, the veteran missionary helps him in every possible way to raise his support. He gives counsel, helps him write newsletters, and speaks in his favor at church services, etc. Eventually the new missionary raises full financial support, and it is during this first year of full income that the recruiter receives a biblical portion for his efforts: 10 percent of the new missionary's income goes to the recruiter during that first year.

It might be argued that this puts too much strain on the new missionary. I don't think so. Everything is new. He is still in the honeymoon stage with his church and supporting friends. Raising an extra 10 percent that first year will hardly be noticed. And besides, some supporters usually drop out after the first year anyway, and since the 10 percent incentive payment to the recruiting member stops after the first year, no one suffers.

The neat thing is that experienced missionaries on furlough can do this while traveling about and visiting their own supporting churches. They are speaking about Wycliffe anyway and potential new recruits naturally come to them to ask questions. Nor do they need to limit themselves to mentoring only one, they could take on three or five or even ten. Just think, at ten recruits, a Wycliffe worker would double his or her own income for a year; possibly just what he needed to buy that much-needed four-wheel drive vehicle or new computer system when he or she returns to the field.

For older members like Jo and me, this may well be the scheme that pays for our retirement. We have the experiences, the stories, the skill, and the enthusiasm to recruit. We also have a diminishing number of financial supporters since our heavenly Father seems to be taking them Home in increasing numbers. Here is a way in which we can continue to serve the task of Bible translation and generate some income as well.

This is such a good idea we are implementing it immediately, today, April 1st.

***

Responses to A Brilliant Solution

I expected a better than average number of responses and comments from readers and I was not disappointed. I got responses from missionaries, both grizzled veterans and first termers; from pastors, mission volunteers, and from board members and mission leaders. But I also got something I didn't expect:

Half of my respondents took A Brilliant Solution as a joke and congratulated me on pulling a good one with such comments as;

"You really had me going for a minute, but a minute was all it took."

"You didn't fool me this time."

"Nice try, Jack, April Fool's to you too."

"You are a nutcase!"

"Your April Fool's Day column is a real 'cracker', I wonder how many you will catch?"

How many did I catch? Well, as one respondent commented,

"I'm sure lots of people are taking you seriously."

About one-quarter of all the responders did not catch the joke and did take it seriously. So, what was their response? Here's where it gets interesting.

Of those who took it seriously only a quarter had grave misgivings. All the rest thought it was a great idea and made comments as follows:

"A creative proposal for fund-development principles and practice."

"The merits are obvious and worthy."

"A win/win proposition."

"I will certainly consider this next furlough."

Those who took it seriously were not the only ones who thought it was a good idea. One-third of those who did get the joke made comments like these:

"Even though it is meant as a joke, I think this idea has merit."

"It has merit, even if we did it on a voluntary basis."

"Your ideas of the last number of April 1st columns would probably work, if only we could get them approved."

The bottom line, 43% of all those who responded thought it was a good idea and worth implementing. It makes one wonder.

April 1

Wycliffe Canada's Innovative Recruiting Plan

Note: I wrote this column a few months before the end of my six years of service as CEO of Wycliffe Canada.

Dear Colleagues,

Wycliffe's *Vision 2025* sees a Bible translation program started in every viable language of the world that needs it by the year 2025. This means growing ten times as fast as we are now growing. No wonder the question on agendas in every Wycliffe organization around the world is, "How can we mobilize the large numbers of skilled, well-motivated workers demanded by Vision 2025?" It is also in the mind of every field worker.

I remember how much work, time and creativity Jo and I expended as we built a team of Canela men and women to be involved with us in the literacy and translation task. In time, we mobilized an inner core of highly skilled people, as well as a large group of good readers to help check the translation for fluency. Recruiting and training took lots of time, resources, and effort on our part. Many of you can relate closely to this.

Wycliffe Canada leadership, along with all of you, at

home and on the field, have been wrestling with the question of mobilization ever since I reported on February's strategic planning sessions. As your leadership team, we finally decided to bite the bullet and make the tough decision needed to put Wycliffe Canada's mobilization plan into action.

If Wycliffe is to be the organization in which a person will work and minister, he or she needs to be convinced to take the first step towards joining Wycliffe, completing preliminary application questionnaire and sending it in.

Our plan, therefore, focuses on bringing as many people as possible to the point of being interested enough in Wycliffe to take that first step. Our biggest problem has always been not having enough well-qualified recruiters "on-the-ground" across Canada to challenge people with the Bible translation task and move them towards involvement with Wycliffe. The key component of our plan is the fact that often the best recruiters are workers fresh from the field.

Although we will still be working on the details and the timing, the basic plan calls for all 400-plus Wycliffe Canada field workers to come home to Canada within a year or so. That is all the translators, literacy workers, administrators, teachers, support workers, etc. Everyone of you will be coming to Canada and will receive training in recruiting skills. We understand your coming to Canada will slow down the work on the field, but we believe the sacrifice will be worth it.

All of you will be given a territory or a city in which to locate and work. The goal for each member will be to influence five qualified people to fill in preliminary application papers and send them in. For couples this would be ten people. As soon as each one of you have recruited the requisite number of people and moved them to fill in the application forms you are at liberty to return to your field assignment. We understand that some of you may end up staying home for quite some time, but we believe you will persist in order to supply the need for more workers on the field. It may also be decided that field workers who prove themselves totally incapable of doing "on-the-ground" recruiting would be reassigned to help staff currently home assigned with processing these applications.

In total, we expect up to 2,000 preliminary applications to result in at least 800 new workers. Just imagine this army of highly trained, well-motivated Canadian workers arriving in field entities! The sacrifice of spending a year or more at home will, no doubt, be forgotten in the joy of having three times as many people active on the field. Doubtless, the rest of the Wycliffe organizations around the world will, once again, be inspired to follow Wycliffe Canada's example.

A number of you may be stimulated to hit *Reply*, wishing to discuss this plan with me. Before you do so, check the date at the top of this letter!!

***

Responses to Wycliffe Canada's Innovative Recruitment Plan

I received the first response as soon as I walked into my office the morning after sending out the email. KG, the wife of the associate director who was to be my successor laughed as she told me the story.

"At home last night," she said, "I noticed my husband

working madly on a long email and asked him what he was writing. He looked up angrily and said, 'I'm writing back on Jack's latest column. This is the very thing he promised NOT to do! He is leaving soon and I'm taking over as CEO, and all this will be on MY plate to handle! He promised me he would discuss any major initiative with me . . . and . . . and . . . what are you laughing about?'

'Did you read the last line?' I asked him.

'Huh? . . . .What? Oh, it's an April Fool's column!'"

Delete! Delete! Delete!

The famous Wycliffe Sense of Humor is alive and well around the world. My Inbox was filled with a much-greater-than-usual response to last week's April Fool's joke on recruiting. Here are brief excerpts from some of the replies:

***

Brilliant! Good joke (but also a great idea).

***

The April 1 date not withstanding :-), we'd be very glad to get involved in recruiting.

***

Thanks for your letter!!! At first, I was shocked, thinking, Wow, this is going to get some reactions. Then I began to think, Trust Jack to come up with something really good to get results. As I progressed I began to think, Well, if coupled with lots of prayer for God to call out more laborers, it could actually get some good results. And then you made me read the date. I was almost disappointed. I was beginning to get into the swing of the whole thing!

***

Actually, until you got to the place where we all had to influence five people you had me thinking you were serious! I would love to get training in recruitment, and I would love to work at it as my home assignment whenever I come home! I am planning to come home for shorter breaks more frequently. This is something I could do for a few weeks here and there!

***

I know it is an April fool's joke, but I think parts of it have potential! See you next year for the training!

***

Oh Jack, that was a GOOD one — really a classic. I was about to forward it to my SIL field office and check the by-laws to see if you're actually allowed to recall personnel. . . You know, I'm STILL going to send it to the field office!

***

Why did you back down? You sure had me going, thinking "*Hold the phone, is Jack high on something?*"

***

This is headed in the right direction. Maybe we can't make people come home and stay home until they've filled their PQ quota (or can we?) but we can think about making recruitment an absolute priority in specific ways like this.

***

I did check the date. But why not do it anyway?

***

Great joke! Good thoughts too. You know, it makes me want to come home and do recruiting.

***

You got me on this one! As I read down through the letter, I started to get a very worried feeling thinking, Oh no, how are we going to spend months at home in Canada this year when Vision 2025-type strategies are at such a crucial stage here?? I was relieved to check out the date. On the other hand, I don't really think it's such a bad idea at all! We field workers are often the best recruiters. How can we best help Wycliffe Canada recruit—and still have the time necessary to get our field work done, keep our families together and our marriages intact, keep ourselves sane, etc.? I wish we could do it all!

***

Thanks for your letter!!! Trust you to come up with something really good to get results!

***

You continue to be my kind of guy. I would be glad to come home in two years and seek to recruit 10 and keep on going. Keep going for it, that's the only way the task at hand will happen. You and I know statistically that people from the field seem to have the best recruitment results. Members could do four months at home mid-term, they could take a year or so off the same as they would for a study leave etc. Keep going for it, that's the only way the task at hand will happen.

***

Sounds like a GREAT idea. When do we start?

***

April Fool's aside, I think this is one of the first examples of the real "out-of-the-box" type thinking that we need if we are going to accomplish vision 2025. It may be crazy to do this but this kind of crazy action is what we are going to need take if we are going to get this job done. I'd suggest we don't just laugh this thought off.

***

Jack, I can't believe I voted for you to be our CEO! :)

***

I got suspicious and checked the date on your message about halfway through it. I love April Fool's jokes! However, the recruitment subject got my wheels turning. We need to do much more to make it easier for qualified people to join.

The date not withstanding :-), We have been struggling with the strong possibility that we'd probably be assigned a desk job, sitting in front of a computer when we come home on furlough. Since I spend all my field time there, at a desk is about the last place I want to spend my furlough. Therefore, we'd be very glad to get involved in recruiting, preferably in the Yukon/NWT, since we've always wanted to visit there.

***

Are you indicating that this big long notice is an April Fool's Joke? I knew it had to be some kind of a joke as it sounded too much like a dictatorship and not like Wycliffe policy. It wasn't really the best of jokes. DP

DP, This April Fools column generated more responses from recipients than any of the other 230 columns I have sent out week by week. Nearly all of them told me they enjoyed the joke, and a surprisingly large number said they were rather disappointed that it was a joke. They felt that some drastic, strong measures such as these desperately need to be taken if we are serious about accomplishing Vision 2025. My reply to them is that I agree we need to do something drastic and show strong leadership but that we would never do this unilaterally from the top down, but rather, as you indicated, involve all the membership in the decision. Remember that I spent 25 years in Brazil as a working member and only five years "stalking the corridors of power". Jack

***

I read your column with interest. I thought, "*Man, Wycliffe Canada is finally waking up*", only to find that what is really needed, is just a joke! What a disappointment! Discouraging! BF

BF, Don't be too quick to pass this strategy off as a joke. You may remember that I promised my readers I would only report on what we are actually doing or planning, not send up a trial balloon to see how people would react. Trial balloons get people all upset for nothing, and destroy the leader's credibility. But this time, framed as an April Fool's joke, I thought it might be a good thing to do. And it was. A very large number of people responded, and most of them responded like you, wishing it was not a joke, but a real strategy. We are in the planning stage for recruiting so a plan like this is still a possibility. Jack

April 1,

A Brighter Financial Future

Note: I wrote this during my three years as CEO of Wycliffe Caribbean

Dear Wycliffe Colleagues and Financial Partners,

One of the neat things I was able to report at last week's board meeting is that Wycliffe Caribbean may someday soon be rolling in cash. Well, the 'soon' may take a few more years, and the 'rolling in cash' may be somewhat overstated, but as our accountant says, "The fiscal outlook is promising." Here's what's been happening:

Early this year I received a report from Avril Foley, one of our Wycliffe Caribbean members, who works with an indigenous people group in Cangosa which has some of the thickest jungles in Africa. Not only is Avril a trained linguistic researcher and a dedicated Bible translator, she is also an accomplished amateur botanist who learned to identify exotic plants in the jungle covered Caribbean island of Marigota where she grew up.

About a year ago, she discovered a unique plant, one never identified anywhere in Africa. It is distantly related to *Aestiferus Calefacta,* or *herba fervere,* a rather fragile plant found occasionally in a small area of jungle in the hills north of Bangladesh in Asia. The African variety, however, known locally as *mbolo ukubila* or 'boil weed' seems to be much more robust and is found in a limited variety of environments.

What makes this plant so interesting is that the Asian *Aestiferus Calefacta*, and its brawny African cousin, generates a noticeable amount of heat. With the proper amount of light and water a mature plant can generate as much heat as a small light bulb. The name 'boil weed' stems from the use the local population make of the plant, putting its leaves in soup, not to eat, for it is quite tasteless and indigestible, but to keep the soup pot warm.

Last year, Avril Foley invited the noted Scandinavian botanist Dr. Olaf Lipro to visit her location in Cangosa and study the plant for himself. He came, verified the discovery, and provisionally named the plant *Foleyferus Calefacta*, after our Wycliffe Caribbean member Avril Foley. Obviously we are proud of her!

But the good news does not stop there. Canadian bio-tech horticulturists who are at the forefront of bio-genetic research have already made some genetic modifications greatly enhancing its heat producing qualities. It now appears the lowly African 'boil weed' will one day make a major contribution to heating homes all over North America.

Environmentalists are in a quandary. On the one hand, they strongly oppose the idea of genetically modified plants of any kind, on the other hand, 'boil weed' may be the key to greatly decreasing the use of fossil fuels to heat homes and businesses, thus reducing the earth's greenhouse gases and the danger of further damage to the ozone layer.

We really hope this will happen. Here's why: Our sister organisation Wycliffe Canada has already signed an agreement with the holders of the patents on our behalf. In exchange for Canadian tax deductions, developers who use *Foleyferus Calefacta*-based heating units in their home and office construction will assign a small percentage of the profits to Wycliffe Caribbean. I can hardly wait!

In whatever way it works out, Avril has already reaped some benefits, receiving a substantial payment for her contributions to Scientific American and Discovery magazines.

In case some of you readers are her financial partners, and decide that she, therefore, no longer needs your contributions, please note the date of this column.

***

Responses to A Brighter Financial Future

I missed both chances you gave me to catch on that this was an April Fool story with both Avril Foley, and Olaf Lipro being close anagrams of April Fool. I still didn't catch on until the end. You are just too good a liar! DH

***

I began to smell a rat when you mentioned Canadian home heating. I am in that business and since I keep current on all developments in that area, I wondered why I hadn't read about it. Better luck next time. CL

Unfortunately, all but a few of the responses to this column disappeared into cyberspace. This last one, however, was the best. It left me scratching my head and wondering. It came from a highly educated (PhD) member of the Wycliffe

International board, a top leader in his field in his own country. Here is his response:

Please grant permission to mention your copyright story as an illustration of how God provides in unusual ways. LP

I wondered, did he really think this was serious? Maybe he doesn't have an April Fool tradition in his culture. Or, more likely, he did catch on, but is now getting me back, making me think he didn't get it? If I explain, he might say, "I knew it was a joke, I just wanted you to believe I didn't get it and get you all worried."

I wrote him back as follows: Dear LP. Permission granted. If you need more illustrations I can invent some more research. Jack

April 1,

Bob Marley and John Wycliffe, Together at Last

"Your kids did a great job!" is something every parent likes to hear. So it is with Wycliffe ex-CEOs. I am feeling good right now. Why? Because I received some welcome news from the Caribbean where Bible translation is being promoted in distinctive cultural ways in several countries.

I had the privilege of serving as the CEO of Wycliffe Caribbean from mid-2001 to mid-2004. It was a challenging job, which makes this recent news about "my kids" even sweeter. Audiences in nine Caribbean countries regularly heard me beat the Bible translation drum. In one three-month period, I experienced a take-off and landing every five days—every flight an international one! In one typical eight-day period in Kingston, I spoke 21 times in churches, on the radio and TV, and in schools. The job also entailed writing 165 columns, articles and brochures.

No wonder that, after all this work, I was delighted to read a report recently from the Wycliffe Caribbean executive director about St Lucia and its famous *Jounen Kweyol* or Creole Day. This event celebrates St Lucia's unique cultural heritage with special emphasis on its French-based Creole language. It is held on the Sunday closest to October 28.

I remember speaking in several St Lucian churches on that special day and being overwhelmed with the enthusiastic reception to my theme of translating the Bible into the local language. This year, St Lucian Wycliffe organizers have an agreement with every newspaper, magazine, radio and TV station to publish or broadcast passages from the Bible in St Lucian *Kweyol* every day in the four weeks leading up to this year's *Jounen Kweyol*. I like this a lot!

The Wycliffe director also reported that his personnel office is being flooded by applications for short-term missions overseas. What is even more exciting is that most of these applicants are pastors of *Bajan* (Barbados) churches.

While interviewing the applicants, he discovered that the churches of Barbados are being impacted by a growing wave of church boycotts. On one Sunday each month, congregations are staying away from churches where the pastor *has not* personally had any cross-cultural missions experience. On *Boycott Sunday* they attend churches with pastors who *have had* some missions experience. They feel a pastor cannot teach them about missions if he, himself, has not had some experience.

Those few *Bajan* pastors who have spent at least three months overseas in missions are speaking to packed out services on *Boycott Sunday*. As a result of the extra offering income, their churches are in an enviable financial position. No wonder short-term missions service for pastors is in strong demand! Although I frequently preached on this theme, I never thought of such a typical *Bajan* cultural response as a boycott. Here's hoping the idea spreads across the Caribbean and over to North America!

Another good report came from Jamaica. As all visitors to Kingston discover when they travel from the airport to the city centre, traffic must flow past a small but famous park in the middle of a major intersection. Elevated on a monument in the centre stands a statue of musician Bob Marley, Jamaica's most famous citizen, who developed his distinctive reggae style of music. His album *Legend*, published three years after his death sold 20 million copies. Marley's music has spread to every country of the world and can be heard from Cameroon to Cambodia to Canberra.

About a year ago this national monument needed major repair and the cash-strapped Jamaican government was looking for private funding for this project. Wycliffe Jamaica leadership saw a golden opportunity to advance the cause of Bible translation. They offered to repair and maintain the statue and the park on the condition that they could place a smaller statue of John Wycliffe near it. Their offer was accepted. A bronze bust of John Wycliffe was commissioned and created by the same artist who did the bust of Wycliffe founder Uncle Cam Townsend displayed in the main lobby of the Wycliffe JAARS training centre in Waxhaw, NC.

This spring the work of repair and development was completed by Wycliffe Associates work crews and local volunteers! Corporate sponsors paid to set up an informative display that is attracting hundreds of visitors each day. The inscription reads, "What Bob Marley did for reggae, John Wycliffe did for the Bible."

It is so great to see these culturally very different ways of promoting cross cultural missions and Bible translation. And what is even better is that "my kids" sent these report to reach me just in time to share with you today, Wednesday, the first day of April.

Note: Unfortunately all the hilarious responses to John Wycliffe and Bob Marley were lost in a change of computers and lost email archives.

April 1,

Palm Sunday, My Father, and Bible Translation

My father had only six years of formal education, not nearly enough to be a Bible translator. That is why I was astonished this week to read compelling evidence that he played a fundamental part in the translation of the Bible into the Frisian language. And even more astonished at how, as a ten-year-old boy, he initiated the work one notable Palm Sunday!

Since I can read Dutch fluently, my 95-year-old mother, a widow for the past ten years, recently gave me a large bundle of old letters and family papers. I was delighted, and have been reading and chuckling over them ever since.

I already knew that my father grew up in the early 1900's in the Dutch province of Friesland, speaking Frisian, a language quite different from Dutch, the Netherland's official national language. Everyone in Friesland spoke Frisian at home, in stores and in the workplace. My father didn't learn Dutch until he started school. Dutch was used for all official situations, in government, in school, and in church. Even though the people in the pews spoke Frisian as their first language, the church services and sermons, the hymns and the Bible were all in Dutch. The younger children in the congregation who didn't know Dutch were, of course, bored stiff.

What I didn't know was that when my father was about ten years old, he and some of his younger brothers decided to play a trick on the *dominee* "minister" to liven things up a bit.

Back in those days only the minister and the organist had hymnbooks. The liturgy at the start of the service called for the pipe organ to play the melody of the first hymn, then the congregation would rise, the minister would stand up in the pulpit, read the first line of the hymn, and everyone would sing the first line accompanied by the organ. Then the minister read the next line, which the congregation sang, and so on.

One Palm Sunday when they knew the congregation would be larger than usual, my father and his little brothers arrived before anyone else. They entered the pulpit, found the minister's reading glasses, and smeared grease on them. Then they quickly slipped into their pew to sit piously awaiting developments.

When the church filled, the service began with the organ playing the introduction to "All Glory, Laud and Honor". The congregation rose, the minister entered the pulpit, put on his glasses, opened the hymnbook, and said,

Wat schorst er aan mijn brille? meaning "What's the matter with my glasses?"

Immediately the congregation sang out, *Wat schorst er aan mijn brille?*

The minister, still looking at his glasses exclaimed,

Zij zijn met vet besmeert! meaning "They are smeared up with grease!"

Everyone sang, *Zij zijn met vet besmeert!*

Suddenly the minister realised what was happening and said loudly,

Dat had ik zo niet wille! "That is not what I meant!"

And everyone sang, *Dat had ik zo niet wille!*

At this, he dropped his hymnbook and glasses on the pulpit, waved his hands and shouted,

Gij zingt het gans verkeert! "You are singing it all wrong!"

And all the people sang, *Gij zingt het gans verkeert!*

A memorable Palm Sunday!

After the service, the minister and the elders gathered as usual in the boardroom, but, this time, not to discuss the sermon. They were united in their assessment of a major problem. The hymn-singing debacle they had just experienced was the final proof that the congregation obviously did not understand the Dutch language they were hearing from the pulpit. Pastors simply *had* to start using the local Frisian language in church services, hymns and particularly in Scripture.

Over the next few weeks they formed an inter-church committee for Frisian Bible translation, the *Yntertsjerklike Kommisje foar de Fryske bibeloersetting,* which produced the full Old Testament thirteen years later, and the New Testament ten years after that.

It Evangeelje fan Jezus Kristus
sa't Johannes dat beskreaun hat

1 Yn it begjin wie it Wurd der;
it Wurd wie by God,
ja it Wurd wie God.
2 Hy wie yn it begjin by God.
3 Alles is troch Him ûntstien;
bûten Him om is neat ûntstien fan
alles wat bestiet.
4 Yn Him wie libben
en dat libben wie it ljocht foar de
minsken;
5 It ljocht skynt yn it tsjuster
en dochs hat it tsjuster der net oan
wollen.

6 Der ferskynde in man, útstjoerd
fan God;
hy hiet Johannes;
7 hy kaam as getuge,
om fan it ljocht te getugen,
dat allegearre troch him ta geloof
komme soenen.
8 Hy wie sels it ljocht net,
mar hy moast getuge fan it ljocht.

I am proud to be the son of the man who did his part to initiate this major Bible translation project. No wonder I became a Bible translator. It's in my blood.

By the way, the name of the minister with the greased glasses that Palm Sunday was Ds. Ap Rilfoolstra.

***

Responses to Palm Sunday, My Father and Bible Translation

So many readers fell for this column I had to post a cautionary note the following week to alert them to the Gotcha.

What a great piece! Thanks for a day brightener. I've made a copy for our Dutch friend, also from Friesland. That's how we came to understand the language situation with Friesland and Holland. J

J, before you make too many copies and send them to your friends, take time to notice date of this column, and also study the minister's name. I think I gotcha! Jack

***

A great story! Thanks for sharing it. I'd like to post in on Facebook for others to read. Any objections to it? W

Recruitment Ministries

Wycliffe Bible Translators

W, sure, I have no objections as long as you take very careful note of the date of the column, as well as the name of the minister! If you don't get it, then I gotcha! Jack

***

I had a good laugh at this one - still wiping away the tears! Maybe we need more small boys smearing glasses to make some ministers wake up to the fact that the people really don't understand them. HH

***

I like your sense of humour! H

***

Prachtig 1 april verhaal. Je had me eerst goed te pakken! (Beautiful April 1st story. You really had me in the beginning.) K

***

You got us all, Jack! I read it to my family the day I got it. Everyone wondered why you added the name of the pastor, but none of us caught on. Then we got your cautionary note the following week and we all had a good laugh when we realized we'd been had! D

***

My dad is quite the trickster himself and has passed that trait on to his two sons (I passed it on to my three sons as well). I have learned to accept and appreciate a good trick that is played on me, so my compliments that you got me with your 'gotcha'. R

***

Yeah, you got me. I feel a little less stupid because the date I received your email was Mar 31, since I'm on the future side of the date line here in the Philippines. I didn't pay any attention to the date in your heading...and it was such a good story. Sigh. :-) Excuse me now while I go forward your cautionary note to all my Dutch friends to whom I had already forwarded your column! R

***

I LOVE it!!! YEP . . . you got me really GOOD. I'm going to share this with a Dutch friend of mine! E

***

Ah, you had me in there Jack - you're such a believable person - usually - till I thought, *Rilfoolstra is an unusual name for a Dutchman.* And it only took me 3 readings of his (Ap Ril)foolstra name to realise I was his name! Good one, Mate! Happy daze, Ap Rilfooled

***

The articles are always great but this one was very touching about your Dad. TH

***

Paul and I haven't had such a good laugh in a long time. But first we also need to clarify. Was this true? The name of the pastor made us wonder. Is this an April Fool's joke? I've had another one today, so I'm becoming wary!!! I'll be waiting to hear before I pass it on. RF

***

Good one. I think I smelled grease towards the end - but thanks for the Rev's moniker anyway! RT

***

I had a belly-shaking laugh out of your description of that Palm Sunday service. Before I had a closer look at the minister's name I recalled that this is the time of year that you enjoy involving your readers in the implications of April 1. Happy April 1 to you too! H

***

Oh Jack, you are too funny. That's a great story on the origin of that story. I love Rev. Ap Rilfoolstra. You're the best!! A

***

Oh, Jack, this one really was hilarious, but also sad when one thinks of this scenario being played out in various places—people parroting responses in church with no idea, or thought being given as to what they're saying— even English speakers in an English service. Even the Lord's Prayer can become a thoughtless routine. And, is the part about getting mom and dad's letters actually true? I hope so. Hugs. You sister, Annie

Annie, Yes, I have some letters. Jack

***

So, was any of this April Fool story true? HW

***

What a great piece! Thanks for a day brightener. I've made a copy for our friend Dirk, whom we've known for over forty years. He also is from Friesland. That's how we came to understand the situation with Friesland and Holland. Americans don't generally know much about Europe unless they've studied extensively or have parents or grandparents from there. We need to be educated as to the rest of the world. JT

***

I am proud to have known your dad. And thanks for sharing this info, I had no idea. Have a great Palm Sunday and Easter. EM

***

That was a really great story! Now are you pulling another April fool's joke? Or is this true? DJ

***

You did get me!!!!! I will be on my guard the rest of today!!! However, now in my naivety I want to know if your Dad was truly a little mischief maker! I think he probably was! Your mischief genes probably came from him just like your translator genes! A

***

This one really was hilarious -- but also sad --especially when one thinks of this scenario being played out in various places -- people parroting responses with no thought being given as to what they're saying -- even English speakers in an English service. Even the Lord's Prayer can become a thoughtless routine. SH

***

That was great. I laughed all the way through. It's amazing what God will do to get His Word out to everyone. What amazed me was the length of time it took to get the Bible fully translated into Frisian. Translations don't always take that long, do they? Or do they? JN

***

Thanks for the story about your father's trick. That can be used for mobilization to make churches realized that peoples groups do not really understand their own national language. HW

***

Okay. You got me again—along with our grandchildren next door. However, this time I had sent your article to a young great niece who I'm afraid will take it as gospel truth. Can you tell me if there is any truth in the article! Is there a Frisian language? (I've googled Friesland and found that it is a place, so at least she will not be misled in that respect!) Is there a Frisian translation? Was your father actually from that part of the Netherlands? Is any part of this story true? LA

LA, Many elements of this story are true. My father really was born in Friesland and he was a mischief maker, loving to play tricks on his brothers, and family. Yes, the Frisian language exists and the Bible was translated by that committee during those years. My mother did give me all her papers and letters. The ministers in those days did read each line of the hymn after which the congregation sang it. And surely somewhere, sometime, some boy did grease a minister's glasses. It's all true, except for little bits here and there which made it such a believable April Fool story.

April 1,

The Last of Jack's April Fool's Columns

Dear Colleagues and Other Friends,

Every April 1st for the past seven years, I have sent out a column in which I tried to fool you. I enjoyed thinking up creative ways to trick you, which, by the way, is much harder than telling true stories.

The April Fool's columns always generated a larger than usual response. Some of you boasted, "I saw through it about half way through." While others had to admit with chagrin, "You got me this time." Your responses, however, were always good-natured, no one ever criticised me for lying so convincingly and so creatively on this special day.

I certainly meant no harm to anyone and thought I was simply following in a long and honourable custom. I had intended to carry on with this tradition, but it is not to be.

In mid-March, I received a phone call from one of the vice-presidents of Wycliffe USA, asking me to stop sending out April Fool columns. He was apologetic about it, being a fan of my columns himself, and explained the reason why he was asking me to do this.

It appears that he has developed a strong relationship with the leaders of a large, rather conservative denomination in the USA. This group has for years partnered with Wycliffe, funding many translation projects staffed mostly by nationals and mother-tongue translators. Recently this denomination had gone through a major internal reorganization, changing their policies and reaffirming their conservative historic roots.

One highly appreciated result of this change is that their board developed a plan with the Wycliffe VP to increase their funding of Wycliffe projects to possibly ten times their current annual donation!

As part of their return to conservative roots as stated by Jesus, "I am the Way, the *Truth* and the Life", they noted that mission agencies and individual missionaries sometimes tend to make themselves look better than the facts warrant. The denomination's board, therefore, set up a committee whose role it is to monitor everything published in print or electronically to make sure it is the plain, unembellished truth.

Unfortunately, somebody told this committee that once a year, a Wycliffe columnist told some of the most convincing and believable lies. The committee went to the WordMan website and my blog and read the last seven years of April Fool's columns in the archives. That is when the chairman told the Wycliffe VP, "Our denomination cannot in good conscience fund Wycliffe Bible translation projects if you continue to tolerate this Wycliffe missionary's custom of telling lies."

When the Wycliffe VP pointed out that this was only

because of April 1st, celebrating April Fool's day in a time-honoured manner, things actually got worse. The committee chairman countered that April Fool's day was of pagan origin and therefore was all the more reason that they did not approve.

After breaking this news to me, the VP told me I could no longer send out the April Fool's column using the wycliffe.org domain or the Wycliffe servers. But, being a personal friend, he suggested I could set up a hotmail or g-mail account and use that to send the column directly from my computer provided it made no mention of Wycliffe.

I thought about the hotmail account option, but realized that if the April 1st column came to you from a different email address and in a different format, it would be a dead giveaway, and the opportunity to trick you would be lost.

So, I am hereby giving up the pleasure of lying to you once a year. This, therefore, is the last of Jack's April Fool's columns.

Yes, I'm sorry too.

***

Responses to The Last of Jack's April Fool's Columns

My month just went flat and colorless! I had been really looking forward to this year's tale! Ah well.... Or did I just fall for this year's version? - that some denomination is increasing its giving by a factor of 10!?! JA

JA, A factor of 10 is not that big an increase when considering the size of the Vision 2025 worldwide Bible translation challenge. Many more areas of work and giving will need to be

increased by a factor of 10 or more, to accomplish it. That being said, I think I gotcha. Jack

Happy to be "got" as long as it means I can look forward to more in coming years! And since I have actually, literally, had brushes with people as rigid as the "conservatives" you describe, am happy to know this instance at least isn't true. JA

***

Liar, liar, pants on fire! You didn't get me. K

K, You are a perceptive man! Jack

***

Nice work. But I was skeptical all the way. I was thinking yesterday of what I might do to trick some friends this morning, and then I saw your email and was reminded of your sense of humour, aware of what day it was. This maybe was the most believable of the ones that I saw, but you make no reference to affirming the truth of your claims, or questioning it as you usually do. So, I'm torn - is it true or 'fool'ish? A denomination setting up a committee to make sure that all Wycliffe publications are the truth? That's crazy, but still could be true, knowing human nature. So, is this column an April fool, or was last year's edition the last one? I'm sure we'll hear about it next week as is the usual case. Or do we have to wait until next year? CH

CH, Thanks for letting me know this was one of the most believable ones. Jack

***

You didn't get me this time. I don't believe it. Next April

1, I will read your email with equal suspicion... A US Wycliffe VP calling you on this? No way. There are churches that believe April 1 has a heathen origin. Yea, right. Next time you tell me that there are churches who believe that the Christmas tree has a heathen origin, or Sinterklaas, or the Easter bunny. Jack, you are not going to FOOL ME! JV

JV, It takes a Dutchman to know a Dutchman. Good for you. Jack

***

I think we've been fooled once again. JS

JS, As long as there is doubt, I Gotcha! Jack

***

Yeah, right! "This, therefore, is the Last of Jack's April Fool columns." You almost had me convinced that there really was such a conservative church group that had no sense of humour. Keep up the good laughs. WH

WH, Congratulations! Jack

***

That's too bad Grandpa. Do you still have the past 7 years of April Fool columns? If you do could you please send me them. Thanks. Love you. SP

SP, I think I Gotcha!

GRANDPA!!! You really fooled me. I felt so bad for you. Still send me the other columns if you have them please. SP

***

Aha! Saw through it right away. It never happened and

THIS is the joke. Right? Or could it be that this IS true? Surely NOT. Thus my first assumption that the column itself is the April Fool's Column for this year—no conservative organization would increase giving by a factor of 10. This was the "clue" line, right? SvR

***

Well, Jack, that was all very interesting since there was no intent on your part to permanently deceive anyone...glad you didn't mention the denomination but I think there are a lot more important things to change in churches than your column. Thanks for taking the attack in the right spirit...you are mellowing in your older age.BZ

BZ, my friend, I think I Gotcha! Jack

Jack, You sure did a great job! You got me good. Go for it. You haven't changed at all and I love it. BZ

You made my day. Jack

***

What is the name of the denomination that funds so many translation projects? I want to verify with them that what you said was completely true or false. Which is it? BV

BV, my friend, I think I Gotcha! Jack

***

I guess I've not been on your mailing list long enough to take note of your annual gravitation into gaming with 'untruths', but just to say that while for different reasons, I stand happily with the nay camp. While it is intriguing to spin a web of words to lure unsuspecting readers into a harmless lair, for me, while I harbour no personal affront to practical humour, from where I look at it, April Fool jokes are better played orally where body language becomes the punctuation. Praise the Lord for this very substantial evidence of committed concern for translation and distribution of God's Word! I only trust that the '*confirmation of historic conservative roots*' will not carry conditions for a 'King James' compatible Canela Bible version! JF

JF, I think I Gotcha! Jack

***

Nice try but the April Fool column appears to continue on. But please correct me if I'm wrong! SM

SM, I guess you will need to wait a year to see. Jack

***

Hey Jack, just don't die on April 1st because nobody will believe you! EK

EK, Good point, I will keep that in mind. My wife could keep on cashing my CPP and OAS pension cheques. Jack

***

Ha, I don't believe a word of it! KJ

KJ, You are a smart lady! Jack

***

This one is the best one yet... you'll get a lot of people with this one. Enjoying your column. DM

Thanks, DM, it takes one to know one. Jack

***

How do we know that you are serious about this and

that this isn't just another April 1 spoof? If you are serious, it would help remove all doubt for you to reiterate your intention on a different day of the year. CD

CD, I think I Gotcha! Jack

***

Well, I wonder if this whole column is an April Fool's? Oh, give me a break. I am appalled. But I guess I am not surprised. I will say no more. With condolences, CB

CB, I Gotcha! Jack

Ha ha! My husband will delight in this!!! Jack, you are BAD! CB

***

Yeah, right. DT

DT, Have I ever gotten you, a top linguist and PhD? The goal of my life. Jack

Actually, you did once. I got clear through it in a totally appropriate state of high dudgeon, and then afterwards thought, Hey, wait a minute ....Enjoyed it. DT

At last! Jack

***

If it weren't for the fact that it is April 1, I would just say forget the "traditional conservative historic organized" church and go for the "emerging" church. Oh dear have I just said that?? And yes, in all seriousness. SW

SW, You are a smart lady not to be taken in by this April 1 column. Many people are commiserating with me in all seriousness, even one of the VPs of Wycliffe International! Jack

***

I must confess that it is only now that I realise you have got us again! Good April Fool's, Jack, that took me 6 HOURS! KD

KD, You're a smart man, a little slow perhaps, but smart at the end. Jack

***

Yeah, well, I'm no fool, and I'm not falling for this one either. I started seeing through it right close to the beginning. You didn't do a good enough job of convincing me, did you of others? LZ

LZ, You always were a smart lady. Yes I got plenty of people, PhD's, members of the US board, an International VP and plenty of others. But I have yet to catch a Dutchman like you. Jack

***

This was so far out that I began to think that this was an April Fool column *par excellence*. Only at the end did I realize that you were telling the truth. It should have been a joke. In a way, it is a joke, but not the kind I like. I'm sorry that there are Christians who don't understand jokes and who can't distinguish them from lies. They must be dull conversationalists, dull speakers, dull preachers. They may not even know how to read a column all the way to the end, which makes them poor listeners = dull.

I'm sorry that there are Christians that seek out the supposed pagan roots of everything we celebrate. April Fool's Day is the least of it. Surely, you've heard that there are pagan roots to the Christmas tree and maybe even to the day we celebrate Christmas.

I'm sorry that there are Christians who believe that the Christian life consists in avoiding all appearance of evil – any possible appearance of evil from anyone's point of view. That's the way of the Pharisee, but it doesn't get close to the things God really wants -- justice, mercy, and faithfulness/humility before God.

I'm also sorry that Wycliffe administrators are so focused on financial support that they submit to absurdities like this. Of course, I've seen it before, but it's sad to see such a blatant example. It will surely be argued that the sacrifice of your April Fool's Day column is a small one to make, when stood side-by-side with all of that money, which we so desperately need in order to achieve our goals. But what will happen if these partners should decide someday that we're a little soft on women in ministry?

I'm sorry that you've been cut off at the knees in an area where you are so darn good. You have made us look like the kind of people that I have always wished we were. For that I thank you very much. Keep up the good work. We need you. BH.

BH, my dear friend, I think I Gotcha! Jack

You're impossible! Maybe that's why I like you so much. You surely did get me. I clearly fell hook, line, and sinker. But I do wonder if you may be driving a little too close to the edge. I know that a good trap requires much plausibility, and, unfortunately, I found plenty of that in your essay. There was nothing in it that I found to be even improbable. Even so, I was expecting some clue toward the end that I had been taken in, but I found nothing, and so I assumed that you were being untypically straight.

Now, I only hope that I was one of a very few readers who were taken in as I was. Otherwise, you may find that you have caused some collateral damage, since others may walk away assuming (bless them!) that you were serious and never receiving the benefit of your correction, as I have. Did you have your wife read this before you sent it out? The upside of this is that you may have hundreds of people all set up to be taken in again when next year's April Fool's Day comes around! I doubt that I'll be one of them. Still your dear friend, BH

***

That, "Yeah I am sorry, too" line is a dead give away!! :) JB

JB, Congratulations! Jack

***

Haha - "April Fools!!!" JF

JF Congrats! Jack

***

Well, Jack. Some things are for a season and they must end. AL

AL, I Gotcha!

***

I've been reading some Mark Twain as bedtime reading...reminded me of you. He was great at stringing people along with just enough fact to drop them with a splash into his tall tales. Keep up the good work. I think your stuff is great...and that's nothing but the truth...no fooling. SVW

SVW, Mark Twain, eh? And here I was trying to emulate Dave Barry. Thanks for encouraging me. Jack

***

Please say this is just your best April 1 article ever. Surely, surely it is not true. AR

AR, "The best April 1 article ever" Well, if you put it that way, Yes. Jack

***

You did pretty good until you said two things, 1) they "returned to their conservative roots", very seldom does that happen. 2) that they would "increase their funding by 10 times". How I wish that would be true and we know they could do it but very few denominations could get all their churches to agree. Now the biggest laugher was that a Wycliffe USA VP could tell you to do anything! Ha! Keep up the good work. I read, enjoy and learn. DB

DB, Good to know that you as a VP yourself were not taken in. The tenfold increase, however, should not surprise you. It will take a lot of tenfold increases in a lot of areas to accomplish Vision 2025 Jack

***

Please tell me this is your April Fool's joke for this year. My husband thinks it is. DD

DD. Tell your husband he is a smart man. Jack

***

You have to wonder about a church/denomination that

would withhold the Word of God from millions because one person liked to run April Fools jokes. It's like, "I am no longer going to fund the purchase of medical supplies to save the lives of millions, because one of the doctors...(you fill in the blank)".Your email does a good job of highlighting this denominations shallowness. I wonder how they will respond? KP

KP, I think I Gotcha! Jack

Ooooh you're gooooooooood! I am so relieved that this was a joke. KP

***

I'm not sorry. It's fun to laugh or smile once in a while, but at some deep inner level, I'm offended too, at good solid believers 'lying' just for a joke. Surely we can find funny things or make up things to cause people to laugh, or even smile, without resorting to lies? Sorry, I'm a stick in the mud. I blame my solid Baptist upbringing! But I'm glad you're so honest, DM

DM, April Fool's pranks are certainly a cultural phenomena. I grew up in Holland where these tricks are big, as well as in England. It is totally understandable that you would feel unhappy at this form of joke, I am a Baptist too but have been a Dutchman much longer. That is why you should not be surprised when I tell that this last column itself was an April Fool's joke. Readers who wrote back are about evenly divided between, "You can't fool me!", and "Oh no, how sad, I enjoyed your jokes so much." Jokes, especially through e-mail are particularly hard to pull off, which is why I do it only once a year. The other 51 columns are all straightforward truth. Jack

***

So, is this all a hoax also that you won't send out more hoax emails? JA

JA, As long as you are wondering, I Gotcha! Jack

***

Thankfully you didn't catch me this time. Keep up the good work. EK

***

Jack, I don't believe you.....:) BP

BP, you are a smart lady. Jack

***

Nicely cloaked, Jack! I'll look forward to another of your valiant attempts at fleecing us when April 1 comes around next year. In the meanwhile, have a great April 1! HG

HG, Well done! Maybe next time. Jack

***

Tch tch tch -- ha, ha, ha. Took me awhile -- but I did catch on before the punch line. So is this *really* your last April Fool's column? -- Tune in next year to find out. SH

SH, I just can't fool an old lady, can I? Jack

***

OK Jack, This one I do find unbelievable!! And I am pre-t-t-y conservative myself. RD

RD, Good for you! Jack

***

I would be curious to know if this is true. I've looked for clues that it isn't and that it is a well-crafted April Fool's joke. If this is indeed true, then Wycliffe USA is letting itself be dictated to because of money. This is censorship. Also, how can Wycliffe USA tell you, a Wycliffe Canada member, what to do? That would be inappropriate. So what's the scoop? If it is true, then I will express my displeasure to the Board and to the President. If it isn't, then congratulations on another good joke! LS

LS, Thanks for the congratulations! Jack

***

Very good. What was the hidden clue, since I recall there's always a hidden clue? LG

LG, This time I was right up front, using April 1 fully written out as the dateline. Also there was an over the top "factor of ten times as much" rather implausible, and the denominations that are so uptight about pagan holidays are usually the smaller denominations that don't think much of Wycliffe anyway. Let's face it, I well and truly got you, as well as a much greater number of other readers than normal. Jack

I have no problem with having been "gotten"! I look forward to hearing about the other responses you got. LG

***

Sorry about this Jack. What a spoilsport! But I accept that you are acting in the name of wisdom, and to give no cause for offence to the church of God. LC

LC, my Jamaican friend, I think I gotcha! Jack

Yu mean to say yu fool mi agin? A how yu can lie so good!? LC

***

Nice try...I didn't believe a word of it! BW

BW, Not one word? Not even the first three paragraphs? Good for you! Jack

No, when I read the subject header, I thought, I bet he's going to try to make us believe he won't do this any more, and that will be his joke. Very clever, though - a self-referential gag. Ingenious! I hope you fooled lots of people. It will make them fall harder for the next year's! (You have "gotten" me before though.) BW

***

Hey Jack. That's okay! I admire you for listening to the requests of others and not causing them to stumble, and remember, "All things work together for good"! BP

BP, I think I Gotcha! Jack

Oh you did! I guess my husband is right, growing up for you was just never an option! Keep having fun and loving the Lord. BP

***

Your fooling faculty functions fabulously, I see. You have left a clue, kindly, just as Conan and Agatha did to allow their readers to compete with Holmes and Perot in identifying it. That clue is in the number seven instead of four (years of April Fool's columns.) Whew, a stay of Fool's Fateful Finality? "Ten times the current annual donation" is another giveaway ... Thanks for the entertaining mystery writing. TH

TH, it's always a pleasure to know I have discriminating readers like you. Jack

***

This is very sad but not surprising - which makes it sadder. Did these denominational worthies hear about the guy who upset his hearers by pointing out the logs sticking out of their eyes or advising them not to throw their (wife's) pearls before the family pig.....? When Christians have no sense of irony, things have come to a sorry pass. PP

PP, my learned friend, I think I Gotcha! Jack

You mean the whole thing about the fundamentalist denomination and its leaders was a ruse? Wow! Sad that it sounds so probable! PP

PP, you, being a Brit, should have suspected April Fool's. But you were not the only one caught by any means. That is the beauty of being devious, use the skin of a truth and stuff it with a lie. But not till next year. Jack

***

I don't believe it. No, really. I don't believe it. AC

AC, You are a smart man! Jack

***

Now is this really a "trick" or the truth? Or are you going to keep us hanging? With my history as a missionary kid and as someone who actually felt I would end up "on the field," I'm choosing to believe it true. If not, then you really got me. J

J, as long as you are doubting, I Gotcha! Jack

***

Wow Jack! I just started reading your column a month or so ago. I missed all those great April Fool's stories! What a bummer! I truly do respect your willingness to set down your pen for our weaker brothers and sisters. Your humility will allow $$ to come in for the Bibleless people! I absolutely love your books and your writing. MW

MW, my friend, I think I Gotcha! Jack

YOU DOG!! GOOD ONE :) MW

***

Jack, is this another one? Perhaps you are going to give up fooling us on April 1...but perhaps not for this very odd reason? or perhaps the whole thing is another one of those April 1 lies? After all, you did say this is the last of them...the last lie? Hmmm. You've gotten so good at it I am not sure ...either you got me once again, or, there are some VERY serious people out there still. Anyway, happy April Fool's day. IW

IW, as long as you doubt, I Gotcha! Jack

***

I'm sorry that I did not know or was aware of the special column and the convincing "lies" that were told therein. Is there any room for levity in Christianity? "A merry heart doeth good. But by sorrow of the heart, the spirit is broken" Prov. 15:13. JO

***

You don't fool me! What denomination would increase giving by 1000 percent? The figure is too round and (skeptic) too large! G

***

Thank you for your letter. We sympathise with your problem. We too have a similar problem - we have been told by Wycliffe UK that we are no longer to propagate the myth of Father Christmas to our children every December. They should only be taught about Jesus. We had been telling them about both, but this is no longer allowed by Wycliffe UK children-raising guidelines. On top of this, at Halloween all children are only to be allowed to Narnia parties. Those dressing up as witches will be fought by Aslan and his army, and duly slain. The consent of their parents will of course, be gained beforehand. (Looking forward to hearing from you next year.) DG

***

This, therefore, is the last of Jack's April Fool's columns. Aw! VG

***

This joke was a dangerous one. It tested how people think about their organization, leadership and colleagues... that is what caught me...I don't think our leadership would sell you, or Bible translation, for 30 pieces of silver.... 50 maybe...but not a billion dollars! Hope you didn't get any angry responses, it would be great to know everyone has high opinion of our leaders...:) FV

FV, Most of the upset or angry responses came from non-Wycliffe readers. Members know their leadership pretty well. There were, however, some notable exceptions, members prepared to confront the President and the Board! Jack

***

You got me Jack! Good one. Sorry I missed the many you wrote in previous April 1st columns. DG

Note to the Reader:

It was not my intention to make this column the last one. But it turned out to be because the following year April 1 landed in Holy Week, possibly even on Good Friday, and I skipped it because it would have been highly inappropriate. The year after that it happened again. The third year, Jo started a round of surgeries which caused me to take a blogging break during March and April. Eventually I began writing humorous columns for the Sunday after Easter, Holy Hilarity Sunday.

I reserve the right, however to restart my April Fool's columns some day, possibly depending on the popularity of this book.

Holy Hilarity Sunday— Celebrating God's Cosmic Joke on Satan

I had a lot of fun in Bible College. This became public knowledge in my first year when several elements came together, crying out for action. Consider these essential components:

- Prophecy was a major focus in my alma mater, with daily chapel reminders of the imminent return of Christ to rapture the Church. We sang of the trumpet of the Lord, and imagined rising to meet the Lord in the air.
- My roommate owned one of the very few tape-recorders in the dormitory and, having worked as a radio DJ could get tapes of sound effects.
- I knew where the school amplifiers and speaker sound system was stored and how to hook it up.
- My daily chore was to scrub pots and pans in the boiler room which gave me access to this off-limits area, through which one could pass from the basement of the men's dormitory to the basement of the women's dormitory.

It was fated that early one morning these four elements achieved critical mass as my roommate and I carried our equipment through the boiler room, positioned the loud speaker at the bottom of the stairs leading to the girls' dormitory, and hooked up the cables.

Ten minutes before the morning wake-up buzzer sounded, I turned the volume to Maximum and pushed the Play button.

Ta-ta-ta-ta-TAAAA-ta!!!! The Trumpet of the Lord sounded!

It took a full 10 seconds before we heard bare feet hitting the floor as girls jumped out of bed. When we heard feet running towards the stairs, we yanked the cables, grabbed our equipment, and rushed back through the boiler room. We stowed the equipment in the closet and were back in our room when the wake-up buzzer sounded.

At the breakfast tables the girls excitedly gave their testimonies,

"I jarred awake and thought the Rapture was happening."

"I wondered when I would start rising into the air."

"I ran into the hall and saw others running about, and I was so relieved to see I was not the only one left behind!"

The apostle Paul called the event of the second coming of Jesus "a mystery," and so was our highly successful prank. It would have remained a mystery if my roommate and I had not succumbed to the temptation to get some credit and modestly allowed the information to slip out that we were the culprits. The staff house committee convened and immediately expelled me. No wait, that was in my second year, and for something else — another story.

Our human ability to laugh at jokes, funny stories and pranks is one of the characteristics that sets us apart from all the rest of God's creation. It is part of being "made in the image of God." God too, laughs. "He that sits in the heavens shall laugh . . ." (Psalm 2:4).

Have you ever noticed that little kids love having fun? My grandkids sure do. For most of my youngest grandson's twelve years, if he wasn't having fun, he was out finding some. That is still his policy. No wonder Jesus, whom His enemies accused of being a party animal, said that we must become like little children or we will never see the kingdom of God. (Matthew 18:3).

In addition to children, two other kinds of people are free of inhibitions and full of fun. People under the influence of a moderate amount of alcohol tend to feel high and have a good time. So are people who are under the influence of the Holy Spirit. The apostle Paul counsels us to be under the influence of the Spirit because there is no danger of the excess and debauchery that results from drinking too much wine. (Ephesians 5:18). There is no way to overdose on the Spirit of God.

Paul often connects God's Spirit with joy. During a serious explanation about the Jewish people's inability to understand the Good News, he throws in an aside, "Where the Spirit of the Lord is, there is liberty." (2 Corinthians 3:12) The Greek term *elutheria*, usually translated "liberty" or "freedom," carries the meaning of "being without restraint to enjoy, to be released from inhibition and constraint to enjoy pleasure." In other words, Paul says, "Where the Spirit of the Lord is, there is good, clean fun." It seems to fit in with Paul's comment on being drunk on the Spirit, doesn't it?

Christians have a lot to be happy about. The resurrection of Jesus Christ was the most deliriously joyful event in the history of the world. It proved without a doubt that He is God and victorious over death, hell, Satan and all his forces of evil. That is why some denominations celebrate the Sunday after Easter as *Holy Hilarity Sunday*. It comes from the ancient tradition of celebrating weeks of *Risus Paschalis* — God's Holy Joke, the Easter laugh.

Things had been going Satan's way right up to the moment that Jesus' scarred corpse rose to glorious life again. On Easter morning, God suddenly turned the tables and revealed that Satan had played into God's hands. What a horrible surprise! Satan and his forces suddenly realised they were defeated. No doubt they smacked their infernal foreheads and groaned, "If only we had known!" But they hadn't. God in His wisdom had kept His age-old plan of redemption hidden from Satan. Paul says, "If they had known, they would not have crucified the Lord of Glory." (1 Corinthians 2:8)

Unfortunately, April Fool's pranks are about the only thing left of this post-Easter celebration of God's Cosmic Joke on Satan. Too bad. In the weeks following Easter, wouldn't it be great if all around the world, hundreds of thousands of church services resounded with waves of laughter at the pastors' stories, and as congregations sang every glad, joyful, happy song in their repertoire?

How about turning these services over to fun loving little kids, or first year college students with a well-developed sense of humour?

The Theological Debate Between the Monk and the Canela

The resurrection of Jesus Christ was the most deliriously joyful event in the history of the world. It proved once and for all that He really is God and is victorious over death, hell, Satan and all his forces of evil. That's why celebrants on Easter Sunday pack church services to the doors.

On this coming Sunday — the one after Easter — attendance will, of course, be back to normal in most churches. But not in all churches. A growing number of congregations celebrate the ancient custom of *Risus Paschalis* — The Laughter of Easter. The Sunday after Easter — *Holy Hilarity Sunday*, celebrates the Cosmic Joke that God played on Satan. Here is the theology behind it.

Up until the moment that Jesus' lacerated and tortured corpse rose to glorious life again, things had been going Satan's way. Suddenly God turned the tables and revealed that Satan had played into God's hands. The Devil was devastated and defeated. The only downcast faces at Easter were Satan's and those allied with him against Jesus. "If they had known, they would not have crucified the Lord of Glory." (1Corinthians2:8)

On this *Holy Hilarity Sunday*, many churches fill this special Sunday service with joy and gladness. As in ancient times, the services resound with waves of laughter as the pastor tells humorous stories, true or not; parishioners dress in crazy costumes, tell jokes, and play pranks on each other; and congregations sing every glad, joyful, happy song in the hymnbook.

In this spirit, I want to tell you about an incident that is supposed to have happened years after Jo and I left the Canela village where, for decades, we lived and worked as Bible translators. The story may not be true, but reading it will give you the option to laugh.

The sandy soil and dry climate where the Canela people live are excellent for growing cashews. We have often enjoyed both the cashew fruit and the nut. It was no surprise, therefore, that some monks built a small monastery on the edge of the Canela land and started a cashew plantation. The monks practiced their religion devoutly while working hard to grow cashew nuts and make wine from the fruit for their own use and for sale. As godly monks, they served both their own needs and those of the community.

All went well until the monks wanted to expand their cashew orchards and had their eyes on a stretch of land occupied by one of the Canela villages. The Canelas were not happy to hear this. They didn't want to move. As is often the case, there was some doubt about whether this actually was traditional Canela land, and the monks were inclined to go to court and have the land declared theirs.

This didn't sit right with the abbot. "These Canelas have the Bible in their own language, they are believing brothers, and we can't just take them to court," he said.

The monks talked things over and rejected face-to-face negotiations in Portuguese, "That would put us into an unfair advantage. The Canelas can't speak much Portuguese, and we can't speak Canela."

After much prayer, the monks decided on a novel approach. They proposed the idea of holding a theological debate between one monk and one Canela, each representing their community. This debate however would be held, not with words, but with meaningful gestures and body language. They suggested this to the Canelas and the idea was accepted. The next day the two representatives met in the shade of a tree on the border of the Canela land.

The monk started the debate by pointing at the ground between them. The Canela replied by stretching out his arms with his hands palms up.

The monk nodded and held up one finger. The Canela replied by holding up three fingers.

The monk nodded again and from his pocket took a small bottle of wine and a piece of bread. The Canela replied by taking out a piece of fruit from his shoulder bag.

At that, the monk exclaimed in Portuguese, "You've won! You can keep your land! The Canela understood these simple statements and walked back to the village very happy.

When the monk returned to the monastery he reported to the abbot and the other monks:

That Canela man really knew his Bible. He was an excellent theologian and won the debate fair and square.

I wanted to establish that we were in the presence of God and started by pointing at the ground meaning, *God is now here.* The Canela countered, by stretching out his arms indicating, *But God is everywhere.* So he won the first round.

I then held up one finger, meaning, *There is but one God.* He immediately held up three fingers meaning, *But He is a God in three Persons, the Holy Trinity.* He had me there.

I then took the blessed sacraments from my pocket, the bread and wine, the Body and Blood of our Saviour meaning, *This is the basic element of Christianity, the substitutionary death of Christ for the salvation of mankind.* I was confident he could not trump that foundational truth. But he pulled out a piece of fruit from his pocket meaning, *Christ's death would not have been necessary if it hadn't been for the sin of Adam and Eve eating the forbidden fruit.'*

"You did well," the abbot said, "but those Canelas are more theologically sound than we had thought. We'll have to look elsewhere for land."

Meanwhile, the Canela reported to people in his village. "First the monk pointed at the ground meaning, *This land is ours.* So I held out my arms meaning, *But where are we to go?*

Then he held up one finger meaning, *You have one day to get off the land.* And I held up three, meaning, *Give us at least three days.*

Then he took out his lunch. When I took out my lunch, he told me I had won and we could stay.

Happy Holy Hilarity Sunday!

Just Write a Short One, Grandpa!

Our family tradition between Christmas and New Year, is to focus heavily on preparing lots of excellent food and eating it. When one of my eight grandkids saw that I was starting to write on my laptop, she whispered, "Just do a short one, Grandpa! We're almost ready to sit down and eat!"

Have you ever noticed how references to food and its preparation *pepper* everyday speech? I was thinking about this during these festive days of feasting family togetherness. Since I love both food and words, and since writing is my *bread* and *butter*, I collected some food oriented expressions for you to *chew* on. They may even be *food* for thought.

We tend to *fish* for compliments and *beef* about injustice. We *butter* up people we want to manipulate, and *ham* it up to get a laugh. We describe a lovely young woman with a *peaches and cream* complexion as a *hot tomato*, or a *hot tamale*, and a brainy student as an *egg*head. A muscled he-man is *beefcake*, a term that comes from *cheesecake*, describing young women modeling bathing suits who say the word "*cheesecake*" to give them the smiling faces so beloved by photographers.

We try to act cool as a *cucumber* when we get caught with our hands in the *cookie* jar, but with *egg* on our face, we turn *beet* red when we are obliged to *eat* our words. We may even have to apologize and *eat* humble *pie* which is not nearly as bad as *eating crow*. We let our friends *stew* in their own *juices* when they disagree with us. We invite the people who can't stand the heat to get out of the *kitchen*. We polish the *apple* for the teacher and eat high off the *hog*. We call the one we love *Honey*, and save someone's *bacon*. We love to have our *cake* and *eat* it too. Spouses look for ways to *spice* up their romance.

A coward is just plain *chicken*. We *table* discussions, *tap* resources, *cook* up new ideas, pull down *menus* on our computer screens, and offer *recipes* for success. We *toast* the bride and groom, *roast* our friends while honoring them at dinners, and cajole people who are slow as *molasses* to wake up and smell the *coffee*. We need a job to provide our *bread* and *butter*, and an unexpected gift is money for *jam*. Some husbands are *meat* and *potatoes* men, fancy foods just aren't their cup of *tea*.

In moments of stress, we may be tempted to drop a few *salty* expressions. Not my problem since I am relaxed having several more columns on the *back burner*. If you don't *chew the cud* on these words, I'll *eat* my hat. Dollars to *doughnuts* this set of expressions is by no means the whole *enchilada*. And after it is over, we may end up all *washed* up and turn into couch *potatoes*.

Okay, gotta go. My granddaughter, now *sweet* sixteen and the *cream* of the crop, is talking *turkey*, using the traditional *carrot* and the stick approach to get me to the table. I don't want to upset the *apple* cart, so will sit down and engage in some serious food consumption. After all, we need to prepare for grim January, with its *fasting* diets and *fat* burning exercises.

Forty-Five Things I Have Learned During My First Forty-Five Years as a Missionary

About Language

1. Hebrew and Greek are fascinating languages, so are 6,910 others.

2. In a mono-lingual language learning situation, the most eager teachers are teenage boys. Thus, the first ten phrases missionaries learn can never be used in public.

3. Never write linguistic data or drafts of translation on both sides of a piece of paper.

4. Missionary couples who have learned the language of some exotic jungle tribe can talk freely with each other about the most intimate and personal things even while in a crowd anywhere in North America.

5. No missionary who can't laugh at himself will ever become fluent in a foreign language.

6. The ordinary working linguist rewrites linguistic papers to the point where he or she no longer fully understands them. That is when they are accepted for publication.

7. When I was a pastor preaching two sermons each Sunday year after year, I spent 90% of my time and effort

studying what the text said and 10% working on how I would present it to the hearers. As a Bible translator, these percentages were reversed.

About Travel

8. When traveling keep TPM (Ticket, Passport, Money) next to your skin at all times. Outside of North America and Western Europe also carry TP.

9. The fewer clothes worn by a passenger in a mission plane, the higher (and colder) the altitude at which the plane is flown.

10. Each motorcycle rider is granted a certain number of accident-free miles. The motorcycle should be sold before that number is reached.

11. In the tropics, a day's hike of 35 kilometres is best done on a clear moonlit night.

About Administration

12. If God had wanted academics to have a vote, He would have given them the ability to make decisions. Instead, He gave them infinite capacity to gather facts and to discuss them.

13. No matter what subject is brought up in a meeting of missionaries, somebody will take it too seriously.

14. An efficient executive secretary triples the effectiveness of the administrator to which he or she is assigned. In many cases the administrator becomes redundant.

15. A specific mission strategy, if practiced long enough, eventually is treated as a permanent core value long after it should be discarded.

16. Since there is no progress without risk, never depend solely on advice from lawyers or accountants ? they are professional risk avoiders.

About Money

17. There is no correlation between the amount of work missionaries accomplish, and the amount of financial support they receive that month.

18. Living below your means lets you sleep well at night.

19. No connection or relationship exists between the final amount listed on a missionary's recommended support income worksheet and the actual monthly support income.

20. The first rule for raising funds for your ministry is "Pray for God to provide." The second rule is "If someone offers you money, take it!"

21. To get instant attention for an e-mail written to a missionary, put "Money" in the subject line.

22. Techno-lust inflames 90 percent of male missionaries and 10 percent of the female ones.

23. The oldest vehicle in the church parking lot belongs to the missionary on furlough.

About Culture

24. Canadians get used to being taken for Americans. Eventually.

25. When dealing with everyone from a mechanics to a government officials, missionaries believe the record of previous actions, not the words of current promises.

26. Sometimes it is extremely hot in tropical mission

fields, up to 45 degrees Centigrade (115 F) in the shade. But missionaries report it is not necessary to stand around in the shade all day.

About Disease

27. Walking all day in a tropical rain will make you wet and cold, but it will not make you sick. Drinking unboiled muddy water will.

28. The missionary family home on furlough delights their doctor when they go in for physical check-ups. He can hardly wait till he gets together with his colleagues and can brag about all the parasites and weird tropical diseases he is treating.

29. A direct, one to one, correlation exists between the need to make a long bus trip and the gastrointestinal distress of the missionary traveler.

About Communication

30. Snakes grow in length by 10 percent each time the story is told. On furlough they grow by 25 percent, unless a spouse or children are present to hear the story.

31. Never, ever, walk away from a crying spouse.

32. Writing a column in which one of the readers' options is to laugh, will be sure to offend some readers.

33. All prayer news-letter recipients read the handwritten note at the bottom first. Since often that is all they read, it is rarely necessary to write a new prayer letter.

34. Never let the facts stand in the way of a good story.

About Other Stuff

35. Furloughs: noun. breaks from duty, vacations Not true!

36. When separated from their parents and living in a children's home, children miss their parents about as much as parents miss their children. This is not a bad thing.

37. Church members tend to put missionaries on a spiritual pedestal. This does neither group any good.

38. Murphy's Law states that "If anything can go wrong it will." For effective missionaries, Satan has added this corollary "Murphy is an optimist."

39. Three of the greatest inventions of the past few decades are duct tape, epoxy glue, and WD 40 lubricant. It's incredible what the missionary can repair with just those three items.

40. Superglue is forever.

41. Never try to *talk* your way out of a situation you *behaved* your way into. (Especially with a spouse.)

42. Do not confuse a career as a missionary with living a life.

43. Spouses have different abilities. I lift heavy things and open jars with my bare hands. My wife finds things I lose.

44. Missionary kids enjoy the widest variety of exotic pets, but only when they are on the mission field.

45. To raise a family that will be happy and effective on the mission field, make sure you marry someone who is just as into missions as you are.

About the Author

Jack's well-developed sense of humour has helped him thrive in an immensely varied life. He worked for a year as an orderly in a psychiatric hospital, a job, he says, helped to prepare him to fill the position of executive director of Wycliffe Canada, a major mission agency.

Humour is essential to Jack as a survivor, who learned to "make it do, wear it out, or do without" during his childhood in enemy occupied Holland in WW2, and the early years of scarcity as an immigrant in Canada. The survival training continued in the first years of marriage as a poverty stricken pastor of a small church, and during the first term as an under-supported missionary in Brazil.

Jack survived being buried alive when a trench he was digging caved in, endured working in manholes cleaning out plugged sewage lines, and drove school bus, taxi, ambulance and an explosives truck. He has also survived numerous car accidents, "None of which were my fault!" he claims.

His humour has often gotten him into trouble – and out again. His tricks, pranks and "anything for a laugh" attitude got him expelled from Bible School. Later he was conditionally accepted as a member on probation for two years by Wycliffe Bible Translators. He survived these events in good humour, eventually being appointed to the board of that same Bible school, and selected to fill several top leadership positions in Wycliffe.

He has taught classes and told stories, preached in churches and spoken at events in over twenty countries in every continent except Antarctica. He is still hoping for an invitation from the Penguin Mission Society. He has spoken in hundreds of cities from Albuquerque to Amsterdam, Brasilia to Bridgetown, Castries to Calgary, and so on through the alphabet, ending in Winnipeg to Willemstad, York to Yreka, and Zanderij to Zeeland.

Jack is as much at home wearing a suit, outlining a proposal in an executive boardroom as sitting half-naked by a smoky campfire swapping stories with illiterate, indigenous jungle villagers.

Jack has several "chief claims to fame." He and Jo, the "wife of his youth" have been married for 55 years. They have three daughters and eight grandchildren who love them and each other. As if that is not enough, they also lived and worked in Brazil for 24 years as linguists, educators and Bible translators. Jack's sense of humour was vital in learning the unwritten Canela language. He could make the Canelas roar with laughter, not by telling them jokes, but simply by trying to say a few words in their language.

When Jack and Jo accepted the invitation to live among the Canela people, there was no approved alphabet and not one verse of the Bible had been translated into the Canela language. When they left twenty-two years later, scores of adults could read and write in Canela, a bilingual education program had been set up, many adults could read Portuguese, a 750 page partial Bible had been translated and published, and there were Bible-reading new believers in every extended family.

Jack began writing a weekly blog in 1993, long before the

word "blog" was invented, sending out his brief story-based essays and reports to 1,400 friends and colleagues on his email list. Many of his postings were forwarded, reprinted in magazines and even translated in other languages. Wycliffe USA eventually asked him to send them a collection of the best columns to be published in a book for a wider audience. The book, *A Poke in the Ribs* sold so well it was soon followed by *A Kick in the Pants*, and then *A Bonk on the Head*.

Connect with the Author, Jack Popjes

Email:
jack@jackpopjes.com

INsights & OUTbursts blog:
http://www.jackpopjes.com

TheWordMan website:
http://www.thewordman.ca

Facebook Personal page:
http://www.facebook.com/jack.popjes

Facebook Ministry page:
http://www.facebook.com/jackpopjes.ministries

Twitter:
@JackPopjes: https://twitter.com/JackPopjes

Other Books by Jack Popjes

Featuring 52 true stories of missions and Bible translation. Buy Online:
http://www.thewordman.ca/jacks-books.html

A Poke in the Ribs

Sample chapters:
- The Missionaries Who Stole the Villagers' Health
- Missionaries Have Bigger Brains
- Oil Drums and Linguistics
- God's Plan—Our Improvement
- The Parable of the Useless Samaritan

A Kick in the Pants

Sample Chapters:
- Jesus and the Giant Scissors
- The Essential Tool Not Even God Can Do Without
- Killing the Dream with Love
- Peace in the Candy Aisle
- Michael, the Real Christmas Angel

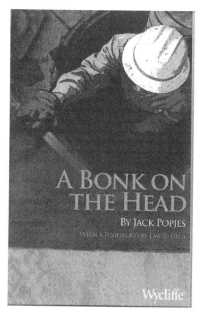

A Bonk on the Head

Sample Chapters:
- The Bible Translation Controversy
- The Case of the Constipated Church
- The Skin of a Hole
- What's so Holy About the Bible?
- Always be Genuine—Even if You Have to Fake it.

Made in the USA
Columbia, SC
09 September 2017